Skywater Publishing Cooperative

for Kathleen, Kayla & Jordan

Skywater Publishing Cooperative
Chaska, Minnesota
https://skywaterpub.com

Library of Congress Cataloging-in-Publication Data
Davis, John, 1953—
Gigs: Poems / by John Davis.
p. cm. — (Skywater Legacy Poetry Series)
        ISBN 978-1-938237-99-7 (Amazon)
        ISBN 978-0-9818279-0-2 (pbk.)
        ISBN 978-0-9818279-1-9 (e-book)
I. Title.
PS3604.A964G54 2011
811'.6—dc22   2009000079

Credits
Connie R. Colwell, editorial direction
Donald Lemke, cover design
Flat Sole Studio, book layout

Photo Credits
Shutterstock, cover
Kayla Davis, page 91

Notes:
"The Biggest Thing" is for Wiley Kitchell.

The line "From my window I play a tiny air guitar" in "Gigs" is modeled
after Jim Daniels' poem "Coming Home from the Hospital after my Son's
Birth."

Acknowledgments

The author and publisher wish to express their grateful appreciation to the following publications in which earlier versions of these poems first appeared: "Brothers," "Here They Come," and "Lowrider," *Between the Lines*; "The Last Summer," *Black Bear Review*; "The Year of Memorizing Poetry," *Comstock Review*; "Prayer," *Cream City Review*; "Saturday Night Overtime," *Cutbank*; "Boxcar of Lumber" and "Halloween Dance," *Exhibition*; "Commute," "This Is Still My Town," *Georgetown Review*; "Frango," "The Singer," *Jeopardy*; "At the Yard Sale," "Bus Ride Home," "Four Tons," "Helping Jack Move," and "The Wide World of Sports," *The Laurel Review*; "She Wore Jeans in Marker's Tavern Parking Lot" and "Thursday across from my Work Station," *Lullwater Review*; "Getting in Shape," The MacGuffin; "In the Basement," *MOTIF*; "45's," *The Nebraska Review*; "Harold's First Day of Vacation," *New Delta Review*; "Factory Worker's Last Request," *New Mexico Humanities Review*; "The Autumn Sedum," *Oracle*; "Letter to the Big Belly" and "Out and Back," *Passages North*; "Day One," *The Pennsylvania Review*; "Factory Gloves," *Pica*; "Legend," *The Plaza*; "Quitting Time," *Portland Review*; "Driving Bullock Home," *Red Cedar Review*; "Harmonics" and "What It Is," *Santa Barbara Review*; "Combustion," *The Seattle Review*; "Early Blues," *Southeast Review*; "How to Fire a Forklift Driver," *Sycamore Review*; "Factory Pull" and "Wedding Reception," *Wind Magazine*.

Frango

Today I'm lonely for light brown rain clouds
layered like frango mint ice cream, a flavor
gone the way of downtown department stores—
boarded up or sold. Saturdays I rode the bus
through Industrial Seattle, pulled the bell-cord
at Frederick & Nelson's, beelined
past perfume counters, ran down brass-railed
stairs, quick right into the Paul Bunyan Room,
spun in my own orbit on a metal stool
until a waitress wearing a black and white

maid dress, hair net, pencil tucked behind her ear
wiped a rhapsody of handprints and perfect
circles of plates and cups, scribbled frango mint
milk shake on her pad. How I spun,
thrumming, kicking the leg of the stool—
a young John Glenn circling the Earth.
Heaven arrived in a metal container,
condensation sliding down the chalice like angel
blessings. In that first moment of pouring
and swallowing, I was the ice cream, the milk,
the frango, the body and bread of Christ and life

everlasting, Judgment Day, the place
where questions about angels were answered,
sugar traveling to invisible bouffants in my body.
I was every rivet of the metal, was sugar
melting ice, was Marilyn Monroe's eyes.
Every vessel in my body whispered frango,
frango. On the wall Paul Bunyan ran
in brown and green earth tones. On the stool
I spooned chunks of heaven with my straw,
swallowed, toasted the first day of the universe.

45's

The old songs come to me sweet as peach brandy:
"Suspicion," "Dawn," "Bits And Pieces."
On the hi-fi I stack records ten deep
just as my sister did, home from college
with bracelets, loop earrings, lipstick and lime miniskirts.
She danced, stutter-stepping like a boxer,
her jabs and hooks rising clockwise,
faking an imaginary foe. She dipped a shoulder
threw an upper cut, as if by dancing
she could outfeint, outhustle and sting
the opposing side of her, my sister
who majored in philosophy, who brought an
east coast rhythm to our home.
She smoked True Menthols, let me click
her stainless steel lighter to "My Boy Lollipop."
I called her Max.
When Mother scolded Max for wearing backless
dresses like Martha and the Vandellas,
Max sneered and ate Red Hots.
She and I hopped to "Rock 'n Robin"
wrapping our fists against invisible doors
my chipped voice high enough for the "tweet tweet" chorus.
We danced, going on like a shoreline.
I followed her lead—a sister's gift to her brother,
a jarring rhythm jostling like a wave,
entering an underwater tunnel that led to nirvana.
If flesh could become water, we would have receded
with the tide. All at once she was gone
like soft rain. I danced and memorized
the skips in "Last Kiss," "Shoop Shoop,"
"Do Wah Diddy Diddy Dum Diddy Do."
Tomorrows stretched out like scars.
She returned and left. Dancing led to running,
led to marathons, bad knees, she in the east,
I in the west. I followed my sister's lead

as if by the dare of dancing I might dance
the dance inside me, might find
how to get the knack between vinyl
scratches and thirty second skips.

Here They Come

I slept with Paul Revere and the Raiders music
racing through me like thoroughbreds,
every song a warning—they're coming they're coming
the years of angst and sex.
It was my first album: $2.50. The drugstore salesclerk
scrunched her face like a rotten peach,
the look she saved for boys buying first Playboys
as if she knew saxophone solos and spicy growls
of rock n roll and what they could do to a boy,
fast fast dance music I snuck upstairs,
removed the needle lint with tweezers,
played the stereo disc on my mono record player
that had only known "Onward Christian Soldiers"
and "Battle Hymn of the Republic."
I skidded across the room. My cat shot downstairs. I knew
I had bought something illegal when Mark Lindsay screamed
"Do You Love Me" and "Oo Poo Pah Doo."
Was it true the band members blew reefer between sets,
drained MD 20/20 outside Northwest dance halls?
Those nights of first facial hairs and translating Latin,
of turn it down, my father's face red as a siren,
I pencil-whapped Using Latin, retitled it Abusing Latin.
When Scipio conquered Carthage, I beat the victory
beat of the Roman bass drum,
screamed stomp and shout and work it on out.
Nothing so mattered as "Louie Louie," not Cicero,
not my Latin teacher who asked Ablative of Absolute questions
on quizzes, then preached opera's absolute hold on Western Europe.
What thunderbolt did the ablative case hold
that Mark Lindsay's saxophone couldn't blow away?
Not grades on verb tests, not after-school track,
not my voice that changed through screams
as I played air guitar and found the nerve to telephone a girl,
not study habits—yeah, habits my Louie Louie ass.
When I was fifteen, rock n roll conjugated my verbs.

The Biggest Thing

Thirty some years ago we were eighteen
and the tough words we used
spread quickly between beer sips.
We were young and dumb enough
to park outside Mac's Tavern,
pay some tavern regular ten dollars to buy us
a four dollar case of beer. We drained it down
in the abandoned World War I bunker.
Maybe the biggest thing was to sing
"Why Don't We Do It In The Road?"
to the gray waters of Puget Sound.
We stumbled home and the wind was talking
through fir trees, telling us to respect the silence
of black space. Maybe we were bowing down
because we were drunk or maybe
we knew the beer didn't care
if we existed anymore,
but we grew silent as fence posts,
regathered our voices, note by note,
sang our silent songs, bowed to our shadows;
ahead the walls, the bed, the 5 a.m. alarm.
But before them and long before mortgages
and aging parents, we laid down on the road,
breathed in the last blackberries of summer,
and for a few moments we owned ourselves.

Barn Dance

After the saxophone solo
blasted beyond the pig pasture,
couples necking in haybales
danced around the scythes and hayfork tines.
Evan and Skye, the polite boys with smiles,
fresh shirts and frogs in their pockets,
grabbed a mug of beer and guzzled. Hiccupped.
Haley, whose job it was to watch the puppy,
inched closer to the chocolate frosting.
Just as Gerald, the lay minister,
knitted his brow in prayer, his wife
loosened her buttons, removed her sweater.
Myron praised the god of cleavage.
Neal praised the god of cleavage.
Oliver lit his lantern and praised
pine boughs blowing, hoping they would crack the
Quonset-hut-of-a-truck of Quinn who was
running for mayor and running his mouth.
Steven, his son, home on leave, stared to the east
ten months before he died dissecting roadside bombs.
Under the night sky the shooting stars burned bright as tracer
        bullets.
Velma later said her baby son was Steven's
which whipped the next year's party into a panic.
Xan was his real girlfriend. She cried for months.
Yellow squash blossomed early those years.
Zany, the black cow, mooed at the milk truck zooming home.

Out and Back

The local lie is that no one knows how much money
anyone makes. Truth is every man wants to date
the redheaded bank teller, hear the whispers
of checkbook balances between her kisses.
I've learned to walk without a song or a bottle
beyond houses where children are praying
their grandmothers' Pekinese will be stung
by scorpions. This road is creased by salt air.
Bits of barnacles grow between pavement cracks.
A man could lose his voice in this wind that rages
against canary grass. I sniff, coyote-fashion, invading
myths the way some countries invade themselves.

Someone needs Elvis Presley license plates
on his Cadillac to burn through traffic.
Maybe he's sober and needs a new obsession
and the sun closes for him like an envelope
of rose hyacinths, or maybe rock n roll armor
is the sweet nothing he uses to fight off fungus.
Walk on. No excuses. No excuse me's.
No one knows confession better than a walker.
No one knows the lies. I walk out and back
like an Aaron Copland score folded over.
The wind off-key through horsetails is boozy

as strudel filling, plenty of Kahlua and butter.
Walk on. Walk like a man till I'm glamorous and my own
gold seal of approval. Walk and the rhythms
in my head float up like a woman's scarf.
I have run naked on this road, jumped into cold
March waves on my birthday, my confessions tessellated
like Escher birds. The wind softens like Galliano.
How different is the scent of pineappleweed
from the glory of a mother, how different
the chocolate clouds, how unrehearsed this
love we mostly find above treeline.

Legend

When day condenses
I hear your lips
flatten and spring
like a slinky.
Sing my name and let me
watch you knot and unknot your hair.
Take me to the delphinium leaves
raging green across your eyes
and breathe into me.
My pores are open
like request lines on oldies radio.

Early Blues

The first guitarists knotted their greasy hairs
around trees, pulled their heads and strummed:
THUD, ka-THUD, ka-THUD-THUD.
After roasting cats and flinging eyeballs
into clay cauldrons, the first guitarists
bit the cat tails in their own gumless mouths,
pulled and twang-twanged early versions of
My cavewoman ran off with my best club
and I sure do miss it.
In time the first guitarists stretched goat guts
and tiger guts from their kid brothers' thumbs
and ker-chunked the I've-got-thorns-
in-the-corns-of-my-bare-feet blues,
surely the first walkin' blues.

Aching hearts, behind in the rent of my false teeth,
and all the woke-up-this-mornings
with baby baby O baby driving me crazy
with your face paints and cave drawings,
all the fires burning for love
and can I stuff white mice in your white hair
for Christmas—all the blues was strummed
on those thumbs and then on the necks
of dead uncles, using vertebrae as frets.
Lord Lord those cannibals, the first guitarists.
No wonder every blues song ends
with somebody did somebody wrong.

Story Problem

Two trains are racing as two trains
are wont to do, one at 50 mph
from Memphis, engineer chewing
on a blues tune, flicking it around
his tongue like a toothpick.

The other train is hustling up from Albuquerque
at 70 mph, engineer longing for his darlin',
singing an empty-saddle song, tipping his hat.
Which train will arrive at Tulsa first?
Memphis is on Central Time,

Albuquerque on Mountain Time, and between them,
heading west, a tornado is expected
though it's guesswork which train track
will be ripped up, and besides,
heading east is a fleecy green sedan

blasting rap, windows down, bass thumping
while prairie dogs, terrified,
hump it back to their holes. In my eighth grade
Rate times Time equals Distance problems,
it was always two honest trains chug chugging,

no railroad company wanting a government bailout
or union concession. We never had prairie dogs
or tornadoes. And there were never any
rapper wannabes distracting the engineer
as you know that engineers are wont

to be distracted down the track at some
railroad crossing in some town where some
baseball player who can't hit a pig's ass
with a banjo, bears down at batting practice
in a semipro league and smashes

a slider over right field into the window
of an oncoming train. And which train?
And what's the rap distraction?
And why do trains want to race to Tulsa in the first place?
We never asked why the trains were racing.

So, between the blues in my backyard someday train,
the darlin darlin my stallion's named Marvin train
and the rapper wannabe Yo homie don't smoke my sedan,
America's children are solving the story problems
of tomorrow. Call them the M generation:

children IM and TM in the AM and PM and listen
to their FMs, or is it their iPods? Their problems
are Greenland and Antarctica melting, raising
the world's waterline by twenty feet. Which Philippine island
will flood first? And how will children resolve the music

of Muslims and Jews? They will create clichés,
find that the good old days are still good, and still
old, find that fewer people ride trains when they
could be burning up fuel and fooling themselves
most of all of the time as people are wont to do.

Brothers

Maybe my brother is building
cottages for jazz musicians and gives
generously to Planned Parenthood.
He cooks hot dogs at Rotary Auctions,
or maybe he's vague, a struggling debater—
the palm reader with matchbox eyes and tight blouse
didn't say, only that I had a brother,
certain as dirt
you've got a brother in the world.

To meet the older brother I never
had, picking boysenberries,
his fingers purple as bruises,
and we match bruise for bruise, wrinkle
for palm wrinkle for chin wrinkle.
Do I greet him like a brother,
do I pass him like abandoned cars,
do I tell him I wanted
an older brother when a father
was too old to be a friend, when I wanted
a hero of my flesh, wickedly cool?

On late night radio I listen
for my brother in the rhythms
and tones of blues saxophone,
a grief louder than mine,
blues that are my blues,
hero to hero, cool to cool,
blowing the faint air of night,
a brother certain as the embryo
figure of a treble clef.

Halloween Dance

The notes the singer
sings to become the song
are forming, are throat-deep,
cantilevered like a steel bridge.
Her fangs and dracula cape
match her cleavage
where a thousand wonders
wander tonight.
Now she dances like nine lives
of whiskey, lunges, spins,
seizes the microphone
and with her voice,
drags the night
like a grease axle
across the dancehall.
Men and women spiked
in Rhinoceros suits
and Zorro masks
chase tequila shooters with beer
just as the singer
wears her smile
like a champagne glass,
bends back her curves,
wrings out the promises
that chew a life.
Is she giving or taking blood?
As the band launches
into a gospel groove,
the Dracula woman
feeds the town with prayer.

Those Songs

I like a good woo-woo baby song
'bout some crazy lady, wavy in lace,
ditsy with daisies, face-pace-chase-
embrace—every line rhymes every time.
She's waiting for her Navy date—her self-made

grenade of a man and he's drinking a half rack
on his way back to his full-rack baby.
She's dressed in black until her Navy
comes back and lands her in the sack.
"Sack" isn't sung in the song

but you know they're on that track.
I like those songs. I don't mention them
to the boys in the band and they don't mention
their hunger for country when we're chugging
through some ear-grinding tune screaming

She grates the flesh off my face
and I dig her teddy bears in a blender.
That's the vampire portion of our repertoire
when the band's injecting its The Infected Needle
persona. The next gig we're heavy with

a Merlot blues or some blackberry-stain-
on-my-dentures tune; music for the moon,
roomy like the thighs of an Earth woman
who catches a man with her mercury eyes.
In the morning I melt into mint tea

and the rosemary rolls in the breadbox.
I can adore any song. Any sound: whirr/ lure—
picking burs in the fur of my Sasquatch loverrrrrr.
Or ick/ick. Or ong/ong. Yeah, ong/ong.
On my way to work give me a headstrong ballad—

a zoom along song 'bout a long dong loser
longing for his bonged-up baby.
No Irish drinking song, just bong/clong
with the strong diphthongs of King Kong
who's been wronged by some hottie from Hong Kong.

She Wore Jeans in Marshall's Tavern Parking Lot

That frizz blond with horseshoe earrings
and four-inch heels crunches Labatt's cans,
her laughter whinnied like a draft horse against country swing
blaring from her Corvair's tape deck.
Frizz cements a pyramid of cans on chrome cans
on doors on lights, an "S" of cans
spiraled on the trunk, sculpts a goat of cans
on the hood, baas and baas, brays when patch cords,
microphones, and quarter-inch jack plugs I carry,
spill out my broken box.
Metal guitar-slides roll under Broncos and Cougars.
Frizz chases twisting high-impedance microphones,
grabs one from Dodge Colt treads,
prances, she dances around my extension cords,
the microphone clutched to her lips,
and her knees like two pistons, they pump-pump,
they pump-pump, they pump and she sings Come on
Come on, leads me to Marhall's door, Darlin
come on, swinging her arm like a windmill,
as red-blue-green sequins shake from her blouse.
She backpedals, heels scraping concrete.
I balance adapters and duct tape spools
in my fingers. Frizz opens me to smoke
and foosball players spinning handles, shows me
the two-butt stage where six of us will sing
"Love Has No Pride," her chapped lips smooth against
my beard. She trots away, spins, the lights on
wagon wheels above her, soft as sequins
on the microphone wind screen in my hand.

The Garden

Before she found the music in her hands,
she would go down to the garden
and rake the sand, the finely crushed
granite sand found in rivers and streams.

She would go down to the garden
in moonlight to bathe in the white
and hear the sounds of waves she had raked
and raked in morning mist.

She would know the back the front the top
and bottom of every rock she had placed in the garden.
She would go down to the garden when snow
inched a line against the shed.

And then she bought the '51 Fender Stratocaster
and punked her hair purple with lime green
racing stripes. The stone, wood and turf
merged among the lichen in silver frost as she

harvested notes along the mahogany neck.
In the turnaround of a D minor blues, she found
herself chording through waves of sound,
gardening the night, the rivers and sand.

What It Is

Bill's spicy guitar-licks slice up the dry talk
and bland voices in the bar, and after Big Jim blows a gritty
melody through his saxophone, the only thing soft in the bar
is the light. Oh how these jazzmen curl and writhe like tomato
    vines,
Bill pumping his head, Big Jim gyrating his sax, eyes wide
as wishing stones. Long ago they abandoned
the sweet sunsets of drumbrushes and honey-flavored piano.
Now when they play ballads, even their echoes
scrape the room. Before the duo closes—Big Jim's mouth
numb as leather, Bill's fingers cramping
on guitar strings—their sour notes
hiss out the open door into the air
past the sticky clouds of day jobs
hiss beyond improvisation
beyond jazz.

Boxcar of Lumber

New guy—Bixby—crucifix and faded overalls
next to me, chews M & M's from his jacket pocket,
lifts wide boards one-handed out the boxcar,
stacks them orderly as brown towels,
says Mercy Mercy.
Already I'm checking my watch, thinking lunch.
Bixby's bald spot is oblong as an avocado
and I'm lifting, thinking guacamole,
tamale, chilaquiles. The boards we lift
are tan as wheat tortillas and I'm
dipping chips from his avocado spot—
guacamole seasoned with cilantro,
and a buxom señorita pouring
margaritas in our salt-rimmed glasses
grins. Her Raven hair is thick as bristles.
She stops, drops her pitcher on my back as I
flap on the boxcar floor under boards.
Holy Geesh, Bixby says. Damn, I say.

And when we lunch on boxcar rails, Bixby
blesses his barbecue sauce and bologna sandwiches,
pulls off cheese layers, calls them sinners,
licks his fingers, flips the pages
of his pocket bible—sugary sauce on Job,
on Nehemiah's blessings.
I carry my faith like an invisible drum I pound
all morning against boards, a faith
that keeps my bologna spiced and crisp
as corn tortillas. Bixby says Oh sugar
when he catches splinters in his fingers—
Oh sweet sugar. I yell shit. We lift. We spit
our promises to the earth.

Day One

Snow outside the factory. Inside, the foreman:
Show me something and I'll move you to doormaker.
Stacks of panels and rails line the aisles.
Everything smells sawdust: forklifts, steel benches, fingers.
My earplugs itch like straw. I squirt glue
in fifty dowel holes, enough for the foreman
to turn the corner smiling, enough for Taylor

next to me slamming doweled end-pieces
into rails with his mallet, to grab my glue hose:
Slow down, Asshole. You wanna show him something,
show him your ass. You make me look bad.
In two days that guy'll chew your ass for something.
Slow down.
Taylor talks with his hands waving

in front of his beard. He's wrong
about the two days. In half an hour
the foreman's back with rags,
grabs the glue hose: Watch me again:
scratch ear, spit chew, squirt, spit,
wipe excess glue with rags—See? Do it fast.

Behind the foreman Taylor scratches himself
monkey-fashion, mouthing Kiss my ass,
his wet Rock n Roll T-shirt sticking to his thin chest.
The foreman turns, catches Taylor's act, smiles,
jerks a thumb to the boxcar yard.

Bob picks up Taylor's mallet. Bob's working
on a beer gut and first mustache. Listen, Asshole,
Taylor's short time. Nobody lasts a week
unloading boxcars of lumber in snow. Just glue my rails
slow. Shitcan the rag and nobody looks bad.
I call you "Asshole," you call me "Asshole." Got it?

He smiles slowly,
gums above his front teeth black as the workbench.
Snow outside the bay doors
falls at twice my glue pace.
I fill holes. Give Bob rails.
Slow. Check watch.
Slow, Asshole. Slow.

Saturday Night Overtime

Rodney yells Rat, shoots nails
with a clamping gun
at a five-inch rat jumping
onto our rails. I drop my door,
bash after the rat with my mallet.

Five hundred rails cascade,
crush redwood panels. Rodney shoots
my feet and I'm dancing until the foreman
chews us out, his left eye flinching
like a turn signal. Between my earplugs
I hum Love it here, Love it here, don't hear

a word the foreman says, his head
shaking like a souped-up Dodge.
I want to rob his pen, caricature
his chin on a panel. The tape
wound around his glasses is brown
as the chew in his teeth. He X's

black ink across a work form,
points to it with fingernails
cracked like dried earth. Our foreman's
so backlogged he can't fire us.
Twenty minutes and the rails are stacked.
Rodney clamps, shoots me into dancing.

I'm gluing doors, watching the rat
jump on the glue bucket,
dance his Saturday dance.

Commute

The bus might as well roll over the fingers and timbre red faces
of beggars. Across from you a mother,
blond, eating pistachios, balances four boys.
You are one of them in a former life,
see your shadow move through youth like vinegar.
No one is breathing. Everyone breathes but you.
You can't believe you forgot to have children.
A radio kicks out headlines.
You are wanted in ten states. Your brother indicted you.
You want the woman announcer
to be gray as the ocean where daydreams
land without expectations of perfume.
The slow hurry in her voice is the exact pace
you want to tumble into love.
Is this the woman who lives inside every man?
Love is won or lost as quick as a bus transfer.
A passenger's laughter so out of proportion
clogs the airwaves and you want its owner to choke.
Look outside. In that house a boy colors
purple lizards on his black bag.
In that car a girl will lose her way
in the dark with love. In that shop
sex is the sneeze of the year. Someone sells
peacocks as watchdogs. You like the colors,
the cackle, the airwaves, the fake laughter
of morning that puts your eyelids on edge.

Harold's First Day of Vacation

Here comes Harold into the factory lunch room
carrying a steelhead by its gills, holding it up,
weighing it on his fish scales—eleven pounds.
Harold grins, his eyes glowing like salmon eggs.
Barbed lures hang from his cap,
same Hyster ballcap he wears cutting
redwood into panels on the band saw.

Rodney, Gene and I bite into Cheetos
and chocolate bars, guzzle Coke, think of sockeye
finning in back eddies. Blair balances galvanized nails
between his upper lip and nose as Harold
pinches the steelhead's pelvic fin,
pokes the tail, Harold's voice
whining like the band saw, telling us his fishing line
wrapped around his outboard engine
before he grabbed the fish with vise grips.

At warning bell, Rodney belches, snaps a beercap
at the steelhead. Does it cry, Harold?
Is this your baby? Want us to bless it?
Blair flicks a nail at the dorsal fin.
Change its diapers, Harold. What are you doing here?
Vacations are for leaving this place.
We're all jealous. I want to stuff a Cheeto
in the steelhead's gills, but Harold
cradles his steelhead out the door.

Quitting Time

Punch my card. I'm gone like steam
from the factory smokestack,
gone, running up Burke Street, down
Thirteenth, lunchbox banging
my bruised hip, gone from pallets
I stack panels on, where I watch
the waltz time rhythms of my
fingers lift, drop-slide, lift, drop-slide,
gone, I'm gone, I'm on
the Lincoln bus, stinking up
the up and coming co-insurance
rookie next to me who grips
his training book like pain,
follows the splintered scars
on my arms. I'm closer, head
out-the-window closer to
my jeep I'll steer. Take me, I'm there,

there, there on Carbon Glacier Trail with full backpack.
Look how spittle on purple monkshead glows like pearly
everlastings. Watch as I hold new growth cedars so
carefully against my face. I shiver like a child
eating nectarines. I measure elevation by silvers
changing to subalpine firs, measure elocution
by the long tones of wind during alpenglow.
Tomorrow let my nipples be firm as rubber bullets when I
butterfly through the sweet cold of Mowich Lake.

Factory Gloves

they are leather
they are strictly cotton
they are spotless
they have grease-stained shapes of goblets
they shake hands like old friends
they shake hands like scowled
men in jousting duels

every glove has torn middle fingers
every glove is groomed
every glove is bound with duct tape
every glove has a mate
few gloves have mates the lefts
find their rights at glove mating
ceremonies in bins

they hold nuts
hold bolts
hold pens
hold dust
saws
drills
and Mars Bar candybars they
know no one they
know everyone and have
memorized every fingerprint they have
ever touched

they are floating they are sleeping they are
standing and thanking sawdust
that covers them in a yellow crust
they say Do not bunch us up
Townships are growing
in our padded palms

We are not colorless and dull
Our back-finger stitching
is blue as sutures of exiled rulers

Thursday, across from my Work Station,

Lazastretti hangs his belly over the belt line,
pulls a comb through his hair,
pulls wooden mutts from the conveyor belt,
stares through bay doors, yells fourteen. His rhythm is
Pull-Even-Stack mutts on a pallet. Cough-Comb-Spit.
Yell numbers, let mutts back up on the belt line
and collide. He jams the machine with a bent spoon.
The foreman comes running. Lazastretti screams
with his hands, grabs his thermos and Gunsmithing Journal,
spits chew at the belt line rollers,
hikes it to the men's room.

Friday, I'm Lazastretti. Promotion or demotion?
He's elk hunting. My boots slide into the grooves
his boots have made for nine years in asphalt.
Mutts bob to me on rollers, bob, turn broadside,
rammed by mutts. I Pull-Even-Stack,
stare through bay doors at beer cans.
Lazastretti's been counting beer cans we chug at break.
Ten I yell. Ten. I don't have to worry about mutts
fitting rails. Pull. Just rub my belly on metal. Even.
Learn to spit, count, yell numbers. Stack.
Carry a spoon.

Driving Bullock Home from Work

In my Dodge Dart, Bullock kicks off his purple
spray-painted boots, keeps his lower lip
plugged with chew, uses Killer and Dude
in most sentences, pulls a Band-Aid tin
from his coat, wants me to smoke ragweed,
his greasy, home grown ragweed. I won't.
It smells like clams. Wouldn't keep a striped eel
stoned three minutes.

He rolls up his window, rolls a joint and smokes,
his thin arms rowing imaginary oars, rowing,
bracing his feet on the dashboard, rowing,
says it keeps him stoned, his cheeks
glowing like rose dianthus.

I shift up the expressway, Bullock yelling
Stroke, Dude, Stroke—a sculler rowing out stiffness
from lifting four ton's weight of garage doors,
his brown hair bouncing off his nose.
Where are the perfect circles
a sculler's oars leave on water?
I want to see Bullock's perfect circles
on expressway asphalt between trucks and BMWs.

The Year of Memorizing Poetry

Truth is I was bored squirting Elmer's glue in two thousand
    doweled holes
per day, living between earplugs, decades of skilsaw screech,
garage doors stacked to rafters. Nights, I drank,
peeled off beer labels, scribbled odes, sonnets—any kind of verse—
taped them to my tape measure. Poetry measured every doweled rail
I ever glued, every life. I checked the tape. Recited.
All spring I thrashed through Stafford, Hugo, glued a rail, Arnold,
Snyder, Sexton, glued a rail, crashed at lunch behind perfect stacks
of scrap lumber, read Hemingway in dusty light.
Maybe the wood began to shrink. Maybe the glue was strong
as the Columbian Gold Ron and Rodney smoked out back.
On a poem I rode piggyback up fishing streams, down fern trees,
smoothed the goosebumps of women with my tongue,
squeezed their spirals of flesh, guzzled whisky so fierce I
might have passed out had I not had a winter sonnet
to sober me. I didn't pass Ron and Rodney my poems
the way a doper passes a joint. Dante, Virgil and Shakespeare
took the screech out of my life. I dreamed with the glue, recited,
found the wide rings in the wooden rails where I was born.

Factory Pull

A pull or two of Mickey's ale, a pull
or three or four will keep me warm on line
adjusting mutts, stacking mutts. I flip
off Jenks, the lifer feeding dowels eight
deep, three deep, eight deep to Rigger One, watch
him spit an amber wad of chew on joints
and screws, keep Rigger One inhaling,
exhaling mutts to the beltline. I grab
my paper bag and pull. He grabs his crotch
with greasy gloves and pulls, spits chew against
my stack, doffs his Hyster cap, turns to spit.

On break he helps me kill the bottle, dips
another chew, tells me don't be old and drink
like him and Tate. Be a banker,
be plumber, be cop or high roller, don't
be dumb and lose an arm or life in here.
I won't let my boy work days or nights here.
Don't be dumb, removes his hat and, scratches
skin as old as goatsbeard lichen, walks off.
After work I drive slowly, drink four beers, five beers,
swear I'll check out colleges. Don't be dumb.
Now's just a temporary thing. My thumbs
are numb as spanner wrenches.
Just a temporary thing.

How to Fire a Forklift Driver

See him as dark rain
that blesses no one.
See him as chaff.
He never votes.
He coughs.
He detests the lavish
designs of riverbeds
and he dreams of creation
in mad languages atop a forklift.
He gives out cheap Halloween candy.
His weekend stories are harum-

scarum liner notes of the devil's
greatest hits album available only
at a 1-800 number.
He traded in his mother
at the Mothers' Exchange.
See yourself as God
or at least a first cousin of God
with sundogs guarding your house.
You grant goodness and miracles
before you eat your corn flakes.
You let sleeping dogs lie.
God you're good.
Grant yourself a low golf score.
Then fire the scum.

Combustion

No matter that the night nudged us west. We crashed
across the fold-out back seat, the hitchhiker and I
laughing up the van in a Utah vacant lot, the air
crusty as unfinished burritos on the dashboard,
and the sandstone rocks outside dark red as deviled-ham.
Erik. Nearly nineteen, hungry to cover the highway miles to
    California.
The combustion of his voice had shoved us through Grand
    Junction,
leaning out the window, swimming the waves of air
that whooshed against us, thrashing his arms in a butterfly stroke.
No matter that we had met only one hundred miles earlier;
we sang scratchy folk songs like the two sadsacks that we were,
his broad brow knitting and unknitting like the moon's soft skin
until we passed out from exhaustion. That was the August
the divorce finalized, and I drove out and back to secure
the few silver spoons and knives from the safe deposit box.
At dawn I trusted the trucks coming towards us not to swerve
their palleted loads over the desert road.
Erik and I challenged every highway curve,
and I dropped all my stored-up whispers, kisses and moans
out the window one by one, watched them spark across the
    pavement.
Whatever furious spirits raged us, we raged with them and
    splintered our voices.
We passed prairies, farms and homes, buildings and bridges and
    the final
pavement slabs before we ran through gray sand to the sea.

Lowrider

has been sawing panels twenty-three years. Almost deaf, thin as
2 X 2's, he laughs at anything, even his name, Lowrider, pants
riding low enough to show the crack in his ass when he bends
over his table saw, eyes a 17-inch cut, slides redwood
through his blade, grinning at the whining panels. 2000 panels

a day. He finds me at break leaning against 2 X 4's, says, How'd
    ya do
last weekend? Ya push em up? My old lady won't give it to me
but once a month. I gotta go across town and buy it.
Used to be a girl on 39th I'd screw. She got
married. Religion and all. Told her she could come

out of retirement if she needed money for her church. Lowrider
    twirls
the slack of his belt like a lariat and lets it hang. The slack
is full of slices from his saw. I give him a cookie. Homemade?
Boy, ya musta really pushed em up. The veins in his arms
are thin as rattails. Lowrider sticks Bardahl and STP oil stickers

on his table. Rodney on clamp yells, Hey Lowrider mon,
how's your old lady's oil, hangin low? Lowrider switches on his
    saw
before the end of break. Rodney flicks
wood chips at Lowrider's crack and Lowrider laughs
most of the afternoon sawing redwood and belt slack.

Prayer

Down at the door factory, Lord,
bless Stubby's beautiful, pitiful coughs
crackling like static through radios.
Bless the chew can rings in Bullock's
jeans' pockets that Rodney uses
as bullseyes for his nail gun.

Bless the dozen donut holes Loman
buys from the snack truck girl,
then eyes her cleavage. Lord, bless her
cleavage when she counts out
change from her change belt.
Blessed be her rouge bright as a STOP sign.

Oh Lord, let no fingers be
chopped in the radial saw and land
fingernails up in the sawdust
pointing to their hands. Bless the hands
sliding panels, greasing valves,
hands lifting, twitching,
hands clenching, hands fitting fly wheels.

Bless nail guns, glue guns, brackets holding
overhead cranes, holding saws. Watch over
wedges of 2 X 4's where Petrocelli
hides his flask. Remember Willard, Ron, Lowrider,
Dago and his Nobody Is Ugly At 2 In The Morning
bumper sticker stuck on the belt line sander.

Don't forget the broken back of Maynard
and the brakes on his fork lift.
May he win television BINGO.
May coffee be strong. May the belt line
be slow. May every sandpapered pair of hands
soften like lanolin when they drive home to
slide up their lover's spines. Amen.

Wedding Reception

Yes Janis I dance I
dance mornings
ten feet above my work
station I slide
quickstep slide quick
through air a fox-trot
with you then we left
two three right
two three over the radial
saws and we dip to men squirting
glue in two thousand
dowel holes We jitterbug
around aluminum chimneys find
Foster hiding behind a sander
pulling from his flask Jerden rubbing out
kinks in his fingers stacking 2 X 6's
I belly roll turn you
fingers light as ribbons We
pretzel above sanders We airplane
over cough cough coughs of Reuben
The music we hum is clarinet rhythmed We
sugarpush over the foreman
timing Basetto who's old
slow stacking eight panel
garage doors We full
spin into night air
your hair light as redwood panels
on my dinner jacket We
dance We
swing dance and
polka You lean
on my arm You lean and the pain
is my hand hammering rails into dowels
The music is forklift motors
skilsaws This is our dance
Take my hand

Four Tons

Your lover pins wedding dress patterns.
You wedge under the sink, head numb
from Friday beers. You cinch
the cold water valve. Cinch it. Bang it.
Cinch. Bang, catch water drops
on your tongue the way you caught

water under showers when you were nine
and wore the plastic shark tooth
your aunt brought from Acapulco, you a cliff diver
diving in the bathtub, your sister
banging the door. You bang. Your lover says
the Pomeroys below are sleeping.
They aren't now. You could hold this job.

Punch in. Wedge under the sink. No table,
radial or rip saws. Swallow water and catch.
You duct-tape the valve, wedge out for break.
Your lover hands you invitations to fold.
You lifted four tons of doors yesterday.
That's eight cars' weight. Today your fingers

can't hold paper. With your teeth you pull
the Magnavox on-knob and football.
Players your age knock helmets. You pound
your knuckles until there is feeling.
When your lover hands you a page of stamps,
you lick and stick them on the Bride's Day cover.

The Wide World of Sports

Tan, muscular types on television turn
double back flips, land
in six feet of water, surface to applause
and a bikini girl handing out towels.
You stand alone
on the arm of your sofa, pull off your sweatshirt
and shoes, suck and release your gut,
bounce on the cushions, bounce,
tuck your chin and flip—two days since you stacked
factory panels and your legs aren't sore
when you land and bounce. You flip again,
bounce across the sofa raising your arms
in victory like the muscular type on television
who's just done a half twisting gainer.
Your steel-toed boots and your overalls still sit on the kitchen table,
your lover's quilting bundled in plastic by the radiator.
Bounce. You haven't polished the candlesticks.
Wave to the sleepy-eyed dog in the poster.
Bounce. Your lover is coming
up the apartment stairs as you bounce,
flip with a half twist
and smack your right knee on the hardwood floor.

After the ice pack, she hands you candlesticks and Brasso,
sits beside you peeling potatoes.
Her thighs are thick as turban squash.
You lean over and kiss. You unknot your sweatpants.
Put that thing away, she says.
We've got my parents coming to dinner.
You rub the candlesticks
as the bikini girl on television
smiles at you, her hair shining like brass.

Getting in Shape

You run because your lover read that running
improves her astral forecast, never mind yours,
your shins aching from your strides on pavement,
your breathing choked like a scroll saw
as you round the fire hydrant on Taylor's Ferry Road.
You've told your lover an hour takes you
seven miles, haven't told her an hour takes you
a mile to Pioneer Pies, a slice of blueberry
a la mode, heavy on the mode, a dunk in the washroom sink,
heavy on the sweatshirt sinking
into water—your guise of running sweat.
You round the Crosswalk Crossing sign,
wadded dollar bills in your sock scratching your ankle,
your eyes on the yellow P's in Pioneer Pies
that glow like beacons. Your running shoes slide
on the graveled shoulder. Your right ankle
cracks over a stone and you roll like a thrown
Coke can into the ditch. You howl and crawl
through brown mud when a tanned woman
aproned gray and blue helps you to her door.
Her thick-with-cookie thumbs
smell of almond extract. You're propped up,
pillowed, ice-packed, eating amoretti cookies,
drinking tea, wanting to live an amoretti afternoon
after visiting a doctor, wanting to have the wide smile
next to the aproned woman and her curves
in her scuba diving picture on the kitchen wall.
You think a woman this pretty should be living in a castle
in Oaxaca. She washes off your mud, her fingers
smooth as blackberry muffins, hands you
the phone. You want your lover
not to answer when you call. She answers.
Will arrive in six quick minutes in curlers.
You shift the ice pack. Six quick minutes.
You roll the words over like ball bearings.

At the Yard Sale

You like the coat rack in the driveway—white paint
on rusting metal. You frisbee your ball cap
toward the seven tarnished hooks. Score.
Your lover turns to a toaster. A woman rolls

hula hoops to her car. The tag on a timeclock reads
works. You grin. Last week at the factory
Bob jammed the timeclock with beercaps and glue,
lunched for two hours. A girl on a tricycle

weaves around bodies, crashes into waffle irons.
You play a kazoo, pull on a diving mask, waltz past
tennis shoes nailed on curved boards—surely the original
waterskis. With a plastic walkie-talkie you Roger

the STOP and Don't Even Think Of Parking Here
traffic signs, watch a boy squeeze his fingers
under the bikini top of a mannequin. His mother grabs
his hand. Your lover pulls you away from six alluring

artichoke shaped lamps: Wait until we're married
she says and buys an Andy Williams album,
fifty cents. You get Black Sabbath.
At home you tape Black Sabbath and stick

the noise in your ears. Across town
a boy grabs pillows in his dreams. All night
mannequins play kazoos, throw diving masks
at coat racks, eat waffles, jam time clocks.

At the Family Reunion

Everyone's going to the five o' clock showing
of Love Story. You tell your lover
and half wasted brother, you find love
every day in the factory when you flip
dowels an aisle away, jamming
the belt of the fingerjointer, ducking and
watching the foreman kick

aluminum legs of the fingerjointer, his pages
of work-orders flying from his clipboard like leaves.
Your lover says you're sick, grabs your beer, departs
with your brother and family. You grab
your reserve beer in the flowerpot.

Sunlight through the chaise lounge
leaves a yellow and brown plaid on the deck.
Carpenter ants on the deck slats
pass on the left. You shove your shoe
in their path. Traffic jam.
You like the power.

Bus Ride Home

The woman wearing avocado
colored gloves and ochre lipbalm

grips the railing over your seat,
asks for your seat, her cinnamon

perfume burning your eyes, the bus
swerving up Marylhurst Drive. She

sways on high heels. You clack your steel-
toed boots, don't answer, chest your thermos.

May I have your seat? she asks. Ten
standing men with briefcases scowl

at you, your ankles aching from
keeping you upright eight hours

at the drill press. May I have your seat?
Looking down, you find her nyloned

ankles brown as caramels. Give her
the seat. You get up but sit down.

Have your feet been clenched all day
in a drill press? The woman digs

a knee in your leg, her face
red as the raspberries patterned

on her skirt. The bus jackknifes,
corrects itself, squeals.

The Last Summer

I hide my mallet behind mahogany panels,
find it each morning dusty
untouched by night crew.
Oil the handle. First whistle.
I rub aches out of my fingers, tape them.

Already dew has dried on rusty cranes.
Three men in a Barracuda
suck a joint, turn up rock n roll.
I punch in, stick in

earplugs, hum. Second whistle and I
squirt two hundred holes with glue,
slam dowels with my mallet,
load dowels. Load-slam-load.

Ron, stoned, hair knotted in a ponytail,
slams beside me, throws his mallet
tomahawk style at the bench, screams
I love this place, laughs and sidearms
dowels at the clamper's back.

Between my earplugs I'm in Tahiti drinking
daiquiris. I hum "Tears of a Clown."
I'm gluing, slamming, going round.
Seventeen days and I'm history.
I'm slamming, waiting for
9:40 break.

Helping Jack Move

7 at night. Beaded snow. You ride in the bed
of Jack's pick-up, bounce past Bronco Billy's and Abbey Rents
bracing an antique pump organ with your back. Your hair
is a cold white crown. Unmatched shoes surround you
in the bed. Against a wheelwell, a wheelless scooter
scratches a ceramic pig.

Jack and his wife and your lover keep warm
smoking Camels in the pick-up cab.
You keep warm pumping organ pedals,
play "Color My World" on cracked ivories—
"Color My World," the only song you know, the prom-song
you slow-danced with Ulrika Somebody as you
rolled your hand along the snow-smooth
white beads on her dress. You pump.

At the stoplight rock n rollers
rev up behind you in a black Nova.
Pump pedals. Your lover at the cab window
tells you Stop. She is coatless, fat arms,
warm against the cab heater. Pump, you pump,

sing to Ulrika, right on Front Street, Ulrika's chest
heaving, left on Wyebeck. You sing, pump,
slow-dance, sway through beaded snow, croon
in your parka past drive-ins and drive-thrus.

Factory Worker's Last Request

Lord, confess my sins to the rip and table
saws. Embalm my calluses. Make the summer
workers touch them. Designate three or four as
pallbearers. Stick my

smokes and coffee thermoses, laced with whisky,
snug against my overalls. Wrap my gloves in
pink suggestion forms as you shovel sawdust
high in my casket.

Roll my casket, Lord. Let me roll on squeaky
wheels between the silent and greasy dowel
fitter. Keep my galvanized smile wide when
company brass and

union reps with funeral faces sob. Oh
Lord, my only Lord, could you mace the foreman,
break his stopwatch, soak it in glue and calm him?
Grant me these blessings.

The Autumn Sedum

The off-key clarinetist will never hit the high C
in "Tequila," but she keeps on blowing
and the marching band keeps on enlarging
its column right corners in the final rehearsal
before school begins. All August

a school daze has been approaching
like a glowworm. The fifth-year senior
has tattooed his forearm with a naked woman.
In the parking lot he is flexing and flexing
until his veins pop up like autumn sedum.

He drains down a beer he bought with fake ID
from Maine. He guns his truck engine.
In a month he will drop out
for hunting season, bag a buck and honk
past the school displaying the antlers.

A refugee from the sailing team picks up
a class schedule and admires the wiry lines
of the girl who's hanging on to the school's
smoothest drug dealer. Her fingers
are getting high and still higher up his thighs.

Tomorrow the ringing bells will summon ghosts
of former students, dead in Iraq. The words
new students are learning will challenge the books
where they live where they murmur where they
memorize graffiti and undress their syllables.

Harmonics

There's a music I haven't mastered yet
but I've watched it—the way the late sun
catches the foxglove, diminuendos across the bell-like
flowerets, ritards into jazz chords.
All night the hums from violets—I haven't learned the sounds.

And there's a care of the soul I haven't mastered
when a woman slides her skin beside my skin,
scrapes away the sour notes of the night
and nourishes my soul with a flick of her tongue.
Her harmony turns the sun back on its dial.

There's a night wind. There's a woman. There's a day lily.
There's a sky made to fit like a shoe.
There's a pale-white throat that's jeweled as a waterfall.
I kiss and fish my way along the good heaven
of this day. Maybe the morning mist

is a boy soprano from the past singing a hymnal of dreams
he never realized. I believe in a woman
rolling naked over grass, the morning dew
filling her thighs. I believe in the jing-jing
songs of the cricket filling up the night
like Ella Fitzgerald singing "A Tisket A Tasket."
We all worry about the harmonics of our voices
instead of our bodies. We worry our voices
will come from the ground like the voice of a ghost.
We don't worry about the streams in our brains turning to pitch.

In the Basement

Each day the dance beat
sleeps in vinyl, lined up
evenly in the basement. It leans
against boxes of chalk
and spare scooter parts.
Dust gathers under
wooden crates of records
the covers creased with dirt
the corners cracked.
Never has "The Twist"
stood so silent.
No one moves to the frug,
the jerk, the pony.
No jitterbug or rumba.
Only the ghosts of
smooch songs
and goodnight love songs
float above the baseboards.
Upstairs, unpacked from plastic jackets,
the CDs bass-thump
into a break dance
and shake the house
down.

Letter to the Big Belly

Dear Bruce: You were this you were that we informed your
fundamentalist sons who ignored you more
than all of their lives, told them you were quite a lover
when they opened covers of your boxed-up dresses
didn't tell them you dressed as a woman once
a month, saw the world double through one-way glass.
Going on a bender meant gobs of pancake and rouge and
hooking a large bra around yourself. How did you
force your watermelon belly into a girdle?
Transvestite was too far for the God of your sons.
But not your God. The love in your fluted throat
was permanent as stone the nights you played
gospel on your baby grand piano you stuffed
somehow between waist-high stacks of newspapers,
records and rusty pans. How did you know
every man needs a song to forgive himself?
Jesus filled up your trailer the way lilac perfume
fills up a dress. You played hell out of that piano.
No heaven could resist you. Jammed some nights
to my guitar trading notes like a litany,
your solos way ahead of mine. Pure as scripture
last time I saw you. Some men run out of wisdom
the way others run out of beer. How strange your heart
should run out on you. What VFW local remembers
you translated the Korean Armistice
into Chinese? What skipper thanks you for opening
bridges, boat after boat for nineteen years?
I guess you know I took your cat. Lived nineteen years.
Another opening? In cat years we'd all be dead.
I'm spreading ashes at your trailer. Probably get arrested.
Are the two of you playing gigs in heaven,
one paw and foot in the air, you in a red wig
and gold earrings, she with a mouse?
Bruce, in some life we're singing in a women's chorus,
holding white flowers, opening our hands to song.
Thanks for playing the world alive. Best, John.

Blues Radio at the Tire Store

Gus on the phone is saying asshole
not mean-spirited asshole, just friendly
asshole calming some customer hassle.
Max the McCaw parrot squawks
in the corner cage biting pistachios,

but true genius here is the guitar solo
spraying from the radio. It's B.B. King.
He's pulling rabbits from a magician's hat.
Definitely B.B. But this is no rabbit solo.
He's sawing a woman in half
then placing her body back, bone by bone,

holding a secret key under his tongue,
going to unlock sadness, give his highway blues
new treads and thirty pounds of pressure.
He's worthy of Houdini in the Detroit River
breathing air trapped between ice.

B.B. the king picker picking notes
the way Houdini picked locks. Foxy.
Squirming out of straight jackets.
No Chinese torture can tame this solo,
certainly not the zoom-zoom of the air gun
tightening up my Good Years.

Gus says I'm good to go. So I'm down the road
with the hassles and the assholes.
I'm facing impossible manacles of morning,
sliding them off my wrists
with the blues.

Gigs

The soundman won't tell us
which patch cords
are plugged in to which holes
which input is in
which is out.
He lectures for 30 minutes
on feedback
and amplifiers.
We remember nothing
and begin plugging in
whatever quarter-inch plugs
come our way.

  ***

Some say her audition voice
is smoky blue velvet
with red lining
but it's a scrub brush
scraping a melody
that wants to lilt
like a lazy cloud.
She's wearing it like some clumsy
moth-eaten poncho
purchased in an all-you-can-fit-
into-a-paper-bag in the last minute
of a Rotary Auction sale.

  ***

We tune our guitars
with plug-in cables
not with our ears.

After twenty-some years
who can hear.
One run-through of "Mustang Sally"
and we discuss blood thinners
and the myth that cranberry juice
shrinks a swollen prostate.

   ***

Before the gig
the drummer, the bassist, the saxophonist
share a smoke out back, renege
on their pact to quit before the gig.
The yellow alder leaves gleam: perfect wig
for the balding saxophonist in the mist.
The trio coughs in 4/4 time before the gig,
the drummer, the bassist, the saxophonist.

   ***

More black leather here
than a Black Angus roundup.
No one dances at the biker wedding
certainly not the groom
who's slamming shooters, shouting
Play "Born to be Wild."
The bride in red and white
is pinching cheeks and leaving
lipstick on necks. The band blasts
into "All Along the Watchtower"
until the sound system feedback
groans out of control.
We unplug everything.

Earl with silver chains
and a handlebar mustache
kicks his way to the stage:
That's the best one you've played.

***

Saxophonist discovers it's an alto
not a tenor that he bought
out of hock.
He's so far off
in his "Louie Louie" solo
that the guest keyboardist
walks offstage
out of the band forever.
A month later she marries me.

***

This LG (lead guitarist) draws pyramids
of plums on the set list,
draws ribbons of leaves.
His eyes are still as graves.
Such guitar fingers.
If he were a silkworm,
he could unstitch the hems
from rhododendron blooms.

***

In the corner, teenage boys are pouring
their fathers' bourbon into Coke cans.
Why else attend a dance?
Their mothers are slow-dancing

with the preacher's cousins, loving the way the Lord
does wonders with a man's shoulders.

       ***

Terri's twitching back and forth
back and forth to the bar
serving fuzzy navels and beer
pocketing dimes and $3 worth

of tips. Little Hot Terri.
The tease of sweet teases.
The LG: Don't fall on your knees
for that be-hind. She's scary.

Terri in a fishnet T-shirt.
Terri nudging up to young men.
Terri nudging up to rich men.
Terri in a suede skirt.

During the sax solo the LG
tells me Terri has a guy
at home. That's why she's a diva
in the bar, plays for money.

       ***

I'm buying he says in a nanny goat voice
and shuffles me offstage to the bar,
says he likes my band, sort of a funky fuck band sound
but with wheels. Man you guys drive it fast,
faster than overdrive. Wanna beer? In the bar's dark
he speed shifts his eyes from the mirror
to his watch, to me, leans into me. This ain't

the place to meet women. All these here drive
pick-ups with Beyond Bitch bumperstickers.
Says he wants to hire the band for a blowout
when he buys a house, gonna fence in

his pool with stolen SLOW and STOP signs,
his way of jabbing the cops for his off-road
traffic tickets. Do I wanna buy food stamps?
He snaps the booklet like a deck
of cards under my chin, and do I snort coke
and blister my guitar fingers on a burner
then wait three days 'til they callus-up good
and can we do "Folsom Prison Blues"
in the next set and can he sit in, he's a great
guitarist he says and do I wanna buy the stamps
and I'm back to the stage, never got the beer.

The band rolls into a slow, shine-your-belt-buckle-
against-some-sweet-young-thing song.
And they're out there, the drag-ass lovers
holding shoulders like the factory
drill press I come to a hundred times a day.
Through the smoke the fast man
at the bar revs up, snaps his booklet
under another chin. I shift,
bend notes along the fretboard,
my callused fingers warm as drillbits.

   ***

To our slowest song
the Marine dances a perfect box step
with his wife.
Someone blows a New Year's Eve horn.
The Marine marches up to the stage.

Too loud.
This is a yacht club, he says.
He's right,
and we're a rock band.
He buttons and unbuttons his sport jacket,
flattens his tie.
By midnight he'll be chiming "Auld Lang Syne."
Until then
Too loud.

      ***

The dyed-blonde in the front row
is mouthing He's fuckin up.
I'm pulling up harps
from my pocket spilling my cellphone
and phone numbers of the repair men
I'm supposed to call in the morning.
I'm pulling up contact lens drops
and a lucky buckeye
before I rip out the A harp
with a penny stuck in the back shaft.
Half the crowd is looking down
on the two-butt stage
examining my life
when my cell phone vibrates across the floor
toward the LG
who's covering for me, soloing
around "There's Good Rockin at Midnight."
I bite out the penny with my molars.
and finally blow into the microphone
to much applause
which I assume is for me.
It's not.
It's for my cell phone

bumping and spinning.
Best floor show ever.

*****

The bald man's head
glows like a white grape
as they slow dance to "Imagine."
He holds her head
a billowy dark red
red grape—
two fruits
squished together
making wine in dim lights.

*****

You want to hit it
and then not hit it—that harmony note
higher than your register now,
the note you used to float
above the LG's melody.

It's like the first serious girl
you dated with straight hair
who gave you your ring back.
You want her in the back seat
with thin arms and thin waist

not the pudged-up hug
she hugs against your
fat frame at your high school reunion.
She comes on to you
with beery smiles.

You nuzzle up to her
thinking you can sing
this song, that you've swum
around this melody
floated the high notes.

All you need now
is to close your eyes,
remember the cold nights
and what kept you warm.
Open your throat and let the tone fly.

***

Why have we let this drunk woman
sing "Summertime"?
The living is anything but easy
as she blares and belches
microphone halfway down her throat.
She's ten measures
behind the song.
Her voice might deflate
the helium balloons
hanging in this clubhouse.
She screams lead guitar lead guitar
at my rhythm guitar
shakes her bottom
against a monitor
until the LG
slices a finger across his throat.
We stop.
The balloons are still floating.

***

In the blue stagelights
the bassist's
navel-length beard
floats like a silk bouquet.
When he misses a note,
he's a flying fish, laughing.
But he doesn't miss
much, certainly not the
costumed Carburetor Man dancing
with spark plugs and fan belts
hanging around his shoulders
like a strand of bullets.

***

The bassist checks his watch.
He'll catch an early ferryboat if we don't encore
but the LG is stirring dancers to a fever pitch.
The bassist frowns and checks his watch.
If he can break his G string or glitch
his amp, the dancers won't want more.
The bassist grins and checks his watch.
He'll catch an early boat. We won't encore.

***

Give the drummer rollerblades to catch up.
The bassist can't find the frets of the song.
The LG tries to slow the tempo with viola tones.
No go. The saxophone begins to writhe
painting day-glo landscapes on the bassist
and the face of the drummer who's decaying
into the roots of the tree where the rhythm
of his drumsticks was born.

The strings of my electric guitar
are wrapping around my arms.
The keys of the unmanned piano are slamming
against our chins as the revolution begins.

* * *

the drummer likes us loud
amplifiers cranked he

mikes his bass drum
mikes his tom-toms

surrounds himself with
seven drums wants

the percussionist to pound
six congas not three

hands me maracas
cowbell for "I'm A Man" breakdown we

high five I
strap on rhythm guitar

stick in earplugs
drummer counts four & we snap

into "Old Time Rock n Roll" bassist
raising his eyebrows—tempo too fast?

I'm strumming chicken-strutting
between congas and keyboard player

young couples bump butts
stage-front center

men over forty numb
from intermission beers in their cars

shake with neighbors' wives
bellies bouncing the drummer

hair twisted like crepe paper streamers
hanging across the hall the drummer

bashes his crash cymbal his smile
wide as the rim of his snare drum

***

On his day off the drummer reads in his garden.
He is the metronome that bends to the basil.
Tired from trimming raspberry vines,
he opens Gravity's Rainbow
and breathes a prelude of silence.

The drummer trims the silence.
He is the prelude of the garden.
Tired from opening gravity,
he reads the breathing rainbow
and bends raspberry-basil into metronomes.

The drummer is reading raspberries.
The basil is the rainbow that opens silence.
Tired from bending preludes in the garden,
he trims the metronome
and breathes in gravity.

***

This morning through yesterday's
haze of rain, I put my dog down
on the metal counter, nodded
when the veterinarian asked if it was time.
It was time. Tumors. Blood.
When the injection filled her,
my dog breathed shuffles
of drum brushes into my hand,
soft pops of percussion.

***

The snow is seamless
a white guitar
waiting to be strummed.

My daughter charges
onto the lawn
in red boots
rolls
flaps a perfect snow angel
dances along the white strings.

From my window
I play a tiny air guitar.

***

The LG is a dead-eye dick tonight
ripping through notes like a cheese grater,
spitting riffs along his fretboard. We lean
back-to-back: rhythm to lead during his solo.

He is running from the rhythm
of the keyboard, splashing past
pianissimo chords.
He is playing his guitar's
inner guitar, racing around a garden
picking patterns of notes as though
they were blooms of violets
daisies and mums
he gives to his wife.

      ***

Dude I brought my guitar.
Can I play my song?
It's gonna be
a big hit
a big hit.
Come on let me play.
It's a big hit.
You can follow me.
Your band needs
a big hit
something big
and I'm big
really big.
I can just plug in here.

      ***

Hey guitarist
my son wants to hear
that bullfrog song.
You know the one
that goes up and down

not the ribbit ribbit
that—you know the one
you know.
I've heard you play it—
and you need to play it
for my son right now.

***

Turn down your amp at a band rehearsal.
It's oom-bap oom-bap—country funk.
I hate this song.
Why don't we play any reggae—we're a reggae band.

Your harmony is way
way off—Don't sing.
Get closer to the mic.
Get back from the mic.

Don't EVER sing.
Bap bap oom-bap.
Turn off the kick-drum mic.
Your rhythm's all wrong.

No "Woolly Bully."
No "Taxman."
That's not how it goes.
That harp solo creaks like a rusty meat grinder.

Did anyone watch the game last night?
What do you call a clean shot—
when you throw a guitar into a toilet
without hitting the seat.

Pull it out—you're sharp.
Push it in—you're flat.
The words are the best part of your song—the only part.
Bap-oom bap-oom.

Hi-hat hi-hat ride.
Did you hear the one about the drummer
who thought
and then thought he was a musician.

You're tone deaf.
Turn off your amp.
Stop singing.
Become a nun.

     ***

After the gig the birthday boy
grins through his wine-soaked daze
says Your band is stinkin good,
plants a wet one on my chin
and stumbles home with his girlfriend.
I coil up microphone cords,
unplug lights and amplifiers,
wipe my chin with a paper napkin
stenciled Sandy Turns 50 Today.

     ***

The LG shows up with a butch haircut
insists we should be a Devo cover band
with yellow protection chemical suits.

Where is the shadow his shoulder-length hair
used to spread in the blue-red stagelights?

The LG's voice is harsh as the plum wine
he swirls in a plastic brandy snifter.
In minutes he's whipping ear-splitting eighth notes.

Where are the mellow overtones,
the slash of waves, the sweeping of the wind?

He squints his wrinkles like a pinecone, says
Poison oak is flourishing in global warming.
Let's rename ourselves P. Oak.

The drummer's dog leaps in the window,
pees on the LG's knee, screeches out the door.

The bassist turns up the reverb on his amp.
The drummer lights a cigarette. A death rattle
hisses from the LG. The band is ready to rehearse.

***

I'm not saying my harmonica married a whistling kettle,
but I warm up quickly, hissing,
praising life, eighth note by eighth note,
beating down the balance of earth and stone.

Tonight I ride the chorus of a song
with my harmonica long past
my solo. Like water coursing through cut rock,
I splash among the wildflowers and shrubs

destroying the blooms. On and on I draw
and blow my breaths, tonguing notes
beyond my scale between earth's outer edges
where silence thrives.

All songs are evolution songs.
I find the note I've wanted all my life
and roll it over and over along the chrome,
the moment of a chorus, a Tyrolean brogue.

It's that note I play through middle age
that keeps me going,
that note of particular paradise
bending it along the edge of light.

The Singer

His voice is thick molasses,
gritted like dust in chaps.
By midnight he burrows mole-
fashion into the microphone, the last
refuge of a drunkard, says
Play it his voice sharp as hatchets.

In the salty stagelights his syllables
weave the path of an angry bull.
He opens his flask, fills
his pewter shot glass, his silt
eyes hooked on a frilled
bodice, his arms reaching for the label

of her jeans. He listens for the distant
questions in her dance steps as the band
drives into a blues, the prelude to silence
every slow dancer feels this night against
his belt buckle. And the singer drinks.
He is the souvenir to angels and ice.

This is still my Town

Forget the rain. Beg forgiveness from the watercress
in the ditch. I grew up in these houses with sons
of veterans, tan with a fast car, cemetery keggers.
The telephone lines dip and climb like Scandinavian thighs.

Stealing was a fever. Steal parkas and gas caps.
Stick pebbles in the hubcaps of the hardware store owner
who accused me of stealing duct tape and nails.
Steal the neighbor's mail, my cousin goading me on.

My friends died in small headlines. I remember
the smell of their sweat from 6th grade
tackle football no pads, hives on their necks
like diamonds. The first time I got drunk

I spliced the wind together like strips
of carnival music. What if I didn't become a veteran,
no dog tags or service number with my name,
became an undertaker, lined my pockets

with amethyst earrings of the dead?
I screamed my theories of love between verses
of car radio rock n roll. My lovers turned up
the music and my face glowed like a landscape mural.

Rain again. Rain forever, even when sun steams the roof.
Envy friends with normal parents. No one has them.
I promised my first wife famous names and answers
and rivers warm with mystery fish. She left.

This is still my town. I go to bed stretching
my backbone or bible or whatever I use for God.
A baby screams herself into a rock n roller. I am happy.
Tomorrows don't rise like dust and settle. Tomorrows open
like french doors. I am still growing up here.

About John Davs

John Davis was born and raised in Seattle. He is the author of a chapbook, "The Reservist." For many years he has performed in rock 'n' roll bands. Currently he resides on an island in Puget Sound, Washington, and teaches high school.

Other poetry titles by Skywater Publishing Cooperative

Bodywearers
Connie Colwell Miller

Whether Miller writes of a red-tailed hawk hunting for mice or a lover's underwear crumpled up on the bedroom floor, her voice is filled with a revealing breath of candor, drawing our attention to the small details in nature and of the body, often showing us beauty where we may not have expected it.

Pacific
Scott R. Welvaert

Two star-crossed lovers, David and Marti, set out to fulfill their dying wish: see the Pacific Ocean. They begin in Minnesota, where they meet at an AIDS clinic, and Pacific chronicles David and Marti's journey through the Black Hills, past Devil's Tower, and to Cannon Beach. Before reaching their final destination, they must first accept their fates and the past choices that have led them down this tragic road.

To learn more about
Skywater Publishing Cooperative
and our upcoming releases,
visit us at *https://skywaterpub.com*
or scan the QR code below